JR,

I wanted you to have this book because you truly are my hero!

I love you,
Leanne

A SPECIAL GIFT FOR

_J.R._

WITH LOVE,

Leanne

December 25, 2003

DATE

Look for these other *Hugs* books:

Hugs for Women
Hugs for Sisters
Hugs for Grandma
Hugs for Friends
Hugs for Girlfriends
Hugs for New Moms
Hugs for Mom
Hugs for Daughters
Hugs for Grads
Hugs for Kids
Hugs for Teens
Hugs for Teachers
Hugs for Those in Love
Hugs for the Hurting
Hugs for Grandparents
Hugs for Dad
Hugs for Women on the Go
Hugs for the Holidays
Hugs to Encourage and Inspire

Stories, sayings, and scriptures to Encourage and Inspire

hugs™

for
Heroes

LARRY
KEEFAUVER

Personalized Scriptures by
LEANN WEISS

HOWARD
PUBLISHING CO.

Our purpose at Howard Publishing is to:

- *Increase faith* in the hearts of growing Christians
- *Inspire holiness* in the lives of believers
- *Instill hope* in the hearts of struggling people everywhere

Because He's coming again!

Hugs for Heroes © 2002 by Larry Keefauver
All rights reserved. Printed in the United States of America
Published by Howard Publishing Co., Inc.
3117 North 7th Street, West Monroe, LA 71291-2227

02 03 04 05 06 07 08 09 10 11   10 9 8 7 6 5 4 3 2 1

Paraphrased Scriptures © 2001 LeAnn Weiss, 3006 Brandywine Dr.,
Orlando, FL 32806; 407-898-4410

Edited by Dawn M. Brandon and Tammy L. Bicket
Interior design by John Luke

Library of Congress Cataloging-in-Publication Data
Keefauver, Larry.
  Hugs for heroes : stories, sayings, and scriptures to encourage and
inspire / Larry Keefauver ; personalized scriptures by LeAnn Weiss.
     p. cm.
  ISBN 1-58229-264-7
  1. Heroes—Religious aspects—Christianity. I. Weiss, LeAnn. II.
Title.
  BV4647.C75 K44 2002
  242—dc21
                                                      2002068840

Contents

★ ★ ★ ★ ★ ★ ★ ★ ★ ★ ★ ★

Chapter 1 ★ Heroes Take Risks. 1

Chapter 2 ★ Heroes Are Compassionate. 17

Chapter 3 ★ Heroes Go Beyond. 33

Chapter 4 ★ Heroes Listen 49

Chapter 5 ★ Heroes Carry the Burden 67

Chapter 6 ★ Heroes Are Courageous 85

Chapter 7 ★ Heroes Take Notice 103

Heroes
Take
Risks

Chapter 1

I am with you

I am with you, and I am mighty to save. I command My angels concerning you—guarding you in all your ways. Because you love Me, I'll rescue and protect you.

When you call upon Me, I will answer. I'll be with you in trouble. I will deliver and honor you. I will satisfy you with long life, showing you My salvation.

RESCUING YOU,
YOUR SAVIOR AND STRONGHOLD

—from Zephaniah 3:17; Psalm 91:11, 14–16

What are heroes thinking when they bravely risk all for someone in danger? They're thinking of the grave risk the person faces if they don't act. What are heroes not thinking when they perform that heroic deed? The possible risk to themselves.

That's not to say heroes act without awareness. It's just that in the minds of heroes, the possible risk to themselves doesn't measure up to the certain dire consequences for someone else if they don't act.

Not every risk heroes accept is monumental

or life-threatening. Not everyone who risks is recognized as a hero, but they are. Risking a job to defend the unpopular truth, risking our vision of the future to accommodate the needs of a sick family member, risking our reputation by admitting a mistake someone else was blamed for—these are the risks that mark the lives of everyday heroes.

What difficult decision are you facing today? What would you risk by doing the right thing? Embrace the risk. Be a hero.

We never know
how high we are
Till we are asked to rise;
And then, if we are
true to plan,
Our statures
touch the skies.

—Emily Dickinson

Amy *saw the form of a teenaged boy just feet in front of her—and in the jaws of the shark.*

Race of a Lifetime

* * * * * * * * * * * * * * * * *

Amy soaked up the late August sun as she sat atop her lifeguard post at the small public beach. The surf was up, and a solitary surfer worked the waves. Local schools were back in session, so most late-afternoon surfers wouldn't arrive for another hour. She breathed deeply, enjoying the soothing sounds of the ocean and the warm breeze.

Lifeguarding was the ideal job for Amy, who dreamed of becoming a champion swimmer. Her schedule at the beach worked well with her training regimen, and the additional on-duty time in the water helped build her strength and stamina.

As she casually watched the surfer, Amy daydreamed about her next meet and envisioned herself being the first to cross the finish line. She opened her cooler filled with ice and bottled water and pulled out a cold drink to quench her thirst. Amy took a long, slow gulp, savoring the refreshment, and wiped perspiration from her face with the corner of her beach towel.

Scanning the surf again, Amy became uneasy and shifted in her seat, straining for a clearer view. She saw the surfer's board but no longer saw the young man. "Where is he?" she said aloud as she reached nervously for her binoculars. Searching the water around the empty board, Amy saw nothing but waves.

She jumped up, grabbing the buoy rope and slinging it over her shoulder, and ran into the surf. She swam with long, powerful strokes toward the bobbing surfboard. When she reached her destination, she located the ankle rope and dove down, hoping to find the surfer still linked to his board.

Suddenly something in the murky surf bumped hard into her. As Amy spun around, horror flooded her right to the bone. The gray object that had hit her was a shark fin. As split seconds took on the feeling of time in slow motion, Amy saw the form of a teenaged boy just feet in front of her—and in the jaws of the shark.

Amy surged to the surface, gasping for air. Then something took over. She gulped down as big a reserve of air as her lungs could hold and dove back toward the shark with ferocity. Terrified but determined to rescue the young man, Amy gathered all the force she could muster and delivered one powerful kick to the shark's snout.

Surprised more than hurt, the shark opened its mouth just long enough for Amy to snatch the surfer and lunge frantically back toward the surface. She draped the boy's body over the buoy and swam furiously toward the shore.

With every kick stroke, Amy mentally braced herself for an attack from behind and fought off panic. She expected razor-sharp teeth to clamp down on her legs, sending shockwaves of searing pain through her body, at any second.

Desperation drove her to swim harder than she ever had in the heat of competition. This race wasn't against other swimmers but against the odds that she and her nearly drowned surfer would survive. The finish line wasn't a painted bar at the bottom of the pool but the safety of shore. Amy gasped for breath and reached deep within herself for the strength to push the dead weight of her victim through the surging tide.

Amy was so focused that the feeling of her foot touching sand startled her. *Why didn't the shark attack?* she wondered as she stood up quickly and dragged the limp surfer through the final twenty-five yards of ocean toward the beach. *He's lifeless*, her thoughts raced. *He could already be dead. Where is the shark?*

Once on the sand, Amy immediately began CPR. Pounding the victim's chest and breathing methodically into his mouth, Amy counted and worked hard. As quickly and surely as the aching pain of fatigue swept through her muscles, a sense of hopelessness invaded her mind as the wet, clammy body under her refused to offer any sign of life.

Still, Amy's adrenaline and dogged determination wouldn't let her give up. Finally, the surfer coughed—at first sporadically and then spasmodically. His whole body shook. Water and vomit gushed out of his mouth. Amy lifted him up to a sitting position and pounded his back, trying to help him cough up the rest of the salt water. He trembled as his shallow gasps grew into deep, wrenching gulps of life-giving air.

Once the victim's airway was clear, Amy laid him back down on the sand to survey his injuries. As she glanced down at his legs, a scream escaped her before she could help it. In her frantic attempt to resuscitate her patient, Amy hadn't noticed the damage done to his lower right leg by the shark's jaws.

The surfer's foot lay separately from his leg, attached only by a solitary ligament. His skin and bone had been severed. He was losing blood fast and was in shock. Amy wrapped her beach towel around his upper calf for a makeshift tourniquet, and the blood stopped gushing. The surfer was still breathing, but she could barely feel his pulse, and he was unconscious.

Amy ran to her lifeguard stand to call for an ambulance. Then she grabbed her ice chest, threw out the excess water, and returned to the victim. Amy grimaced as she took firm hold of the foot and gave one forceful yank. The ligament snapped, and she packed the severed foot in the ice and closed the cooler.

Shuddering with horror at the gruesomeness of her task, Amy heard sirens and turned to see the ambulance approaching. Paramedics rushed to the scene and checked the victim's vital signs. They administered oxygen and carried the surfer on a stretcher into the waiting emergency vehicle. It all happened so quickly that Amy hardly uttered anything but a few bits of vital information to the medical team.

When the ambulance pulled away, two police officers arrived to check on Amy and gather information for their report. Dazed, exhausted, and overwhelmed, Amy finally allowed herself to react. She began to tremble, and she sat down quickly, feeling her knees start to give out beneath her. In the aftermath of trauma, tears now flowed freely down her cheeks.

A small band of surfers just arriving at the beach also gathered around as Amy explained to the officers what had happened. Amy wrapped herself in a beach towel loaned to her by one of the surfers and shivered in disbelief as she told of her terrifying encounter with the shark.

When she had given police the information they needed, Amy persuaded them to take her to the hospital to follow up on the shark-attack victim. When they arrived, she rushed into the emergency-room waiting area just as the receptionist was telling other officers that the boy had been rushed to surgery. A team of surgeons was being hastily assembled for the tedious and difficult task of trying to successfully reattach the foot.

Several hours later, the surgery was completed. Now only time would tell whether the operation had been a success. Amy learned that the boy's name was Tom and that he was only sixteen. Throughout his recovery, Amy kept in touch and frequently visited him in the hospital, encouraging him to hope for the best and focus on recovery.

Six weeks later, Amy was honored in a ceremony outside the small city hall of her seaside village. She listened appreciatively as local dignitaries, police, rescue workers, and doctors praised her rescue effort. Amy's courage, quick thinking, and swift action had saved Tom's life and his foot.

Amy's favorite part of the ceremony, however, was when she looked across the parking lot and spotted Tom, who was recovering well and, miraculously, was on his way to regaining full use of his right foot. Their eyes met—surfer and lifeguard, victim and rescuer. Tom's expression spoke a gratitude that only a person who had been given a second chance at life could communicate and that only a hero could understand. Amy could ask for no better reward.

Heroes
Are
Compassionate

Chapter

2

With everlasting kindn

With everlasting kindness, I'm compassionate and loving toward you. Let Me enlighten the eyes of your heart so you'll know the hope I've destined for you. Don't just think about yourself; be considerate of others.

Show mercy and compassion to one another. As you continue to commit everything you do to Me, I'll make you successful.

COMPASSIONATELY,
YOUR GOD OF ALL COMFORT

—from Isaiah 54:8; Ephesians 1:18–19; Philippians 2:3–4; Zechariah 7:9; Proverbs 16:3

Heroes possess a wellspring of compassion, and they demonstrate that compassion through heroic actions and words.

With heroic compassion, Abraham Lincoln penned the Gettysburg address. Florence Nightingale dressed wounds in the Crimea. Martin Luther King Jr. voiced a dream of liberty for the oppressed.

Compassion motivates people to perform heroic acts of bravery, kindness, and generosity. It's the force that moves rescuers to brave the worst of storms to reach helpless victims and relief workers to travel to *inspirational message*

Third-World countries to provide relief after tragedy.

Compassion also is manifested in quieter but no less heroic ways. Because they feel the pain of others, heroes cry…heroes pray…heroes overcome obstacles…and heroes persevere.

Heroic compassion makes a difference in the lives of others. Perhaps someone near you is hurting or in need. Perhaps that person's wounds can be healed, his hurts soothed, her life changed by a compassionate word or act from a hero like you.

God is a Specialist
at making something
useful and beautiful
out of something
broken and confused.

—Charles R. Swindoll

He *didn't know if it had been the medicine or the angioplasty, but something had definitely affected his heart.*

The Heart of a Hero

* * * * * * * * * * * * * * * * * * * *

The gray, wintry weather outside seemed to penetrate the window of the semiprivate hospital room through half-pulled shades. Jack felt as gloomy as the view. Severe chest pains had brought him to the emergency room the evening before, and now he lay in bed in the hospital's coronary care unit.

Angioplasty...me?...this can't be... Jack struggled to comprehend his situation. Although medication dulled his pain to a vague discomfort, the drugs failed to relieve the nagging irritation that his schedule, usually crammed with business meetings, was now out of his control. *Today is Monday...by Thursday morning I have to be on a plane headed for Chicago to*

put out a corporate fire in our Midwest regional office. He grimaced, teeth clenched, at the aggravation of this unscheduled event.

He had already called the office and instructed his assistant not to let anyone know about his emergency. He wanted no visitors, no calls, no flowers or cards—no sympathy. All Jack wanted was to recover quickly so he could get back to his own agenda. He shut his eyes to block out the two other people in the room. I can't believe there were no private rooms available, he grumbled to himself.

But his restlessness wouldn't let his eyes remain closed. His gaze skipped around the room and landed on his roommate. The elderly man rarely stirred as he gasped to get air through the oxygen mask tethered to his face. He seemed quite ill, and his diminutive wife looked weary as she laced her bony fingers affectionately with his.

Something about the old couple struck him hard. The tenderness and love they felt for one another was unmistakable. There was a new, strange sensation in Jack's malfunctioning heart. All of his success, money, and reputation could never afford him what this modest little couple so obviously had.

Jack had never had time for a wife or family. His college education had launched him from business school into a hectic career that consumed his time and emotions. He wondered, when the end of his life came, would anyone look at him with such longing and concern? Would anyone stay by his side, hold his hand, pray for his recovery, and mourn his loss? If his heart procedure turned out badly—and he would be a fool not to at least consider that possibility—he knew he would die an incredibly poor man.

Suddenly he could hardly bear that thought. It made him uncomfortable. It made him grumpy. He pushed the thought away and tried to distract his mind with business priorities. But his gaze and his thoughts turned again to the man in the next bed and the woman beside him. This time they reminded him of his own aging parents two thousand miles away. A wave of nostalgia and regret flooded him as he reflected on how little time he had spent with them over the years and how lonely they must be.

Jack felt he needed to speak to the woman across the room. "How's your husband, Emma?"

The elderly woman looked up, startled. "I heard the nurse call you Emma," he explained, realizing for the first time that they were more a part of his world than he was of theirs.

The answer satisfied her, and she looked back toward her husband, sadly. "Not good," she replied. "John isn't well. He had a pacemaker put in, but he's not responding well. I'm so worried," she admitted, then dissolved into silent tears.

While Jack tried to decide what he could say to comfort Emma, orderlies came with a gurney to wheel him away for his procedure. "See you later," he said weakly to Emma. Jack rarely prayed these days, but this was certainly the time to reach back and pull up some spiritual strength both for himself and for an elderly couple all alone. "I'll pray for you both," Jack promised as he was wheeled out the door.

As they passed into the hallway, Jack studied the name below his own posted outside the room. Vanderhassen. An unusual name, he thought. Vanderhassen. Vanderhassen. Suddenly it felt important to remember that name.

God, please bless Emma and John Vanderhassen, Jack prayed silently as he was wheeled onto the elevator. *And God...please help me through this too.*

It was a prayer God would answer.

The doctors pronounced Jack's procedure a complete success. Already the pain in his chest was gone, and he was feeling relieved and deeply grateful. He was looking forward to seeing Emma and John again.

But when he got back to the room, it was empty. The bed next to his had been stripped of its sheets, and none of John's personal items remained in the room. With a growing sense of dread, Jack questioned the nurse: "What happened to the old couple?"

"The man died around noon while you were with the doctor," the nurse answered indifferently.

Tears unexpectedly flooded Jack's eyes. He could neither explain nor contain his grief. Somehow, the death of the old man who had been so dearly loved left him feeling emptier than he could have imagined. Suddenly he felt a strong need to talk to his parents.

Jack found his cell phone and called his parents, letting them know about his emergency and that everything would be OK. "Jack, you should have called. I would have added this procedure to my prayers for you," his mom said.

"I know," Jack replied. "See you in a couple of days." Before his mom could respond, Jack said good-bye, tears filling his eyes. "I'll pray for you. I love you."

He didn't know if it had been the medicine or the angioplasty, but something had definitely affected his heart. He liked the way it felt. He hoped it would last forever.

The next morning Jack waited anxiously for the doctor to sign off on his release. Suddenly he knew what he wanted to do. The deep needs of this elderly woman had awakened in him the quality that all heroes seem to possess—compassion.

Grabbing his cell phone, he speed-dialed his office and left a message for his assistant. "I'm doing OK. Everything went well, and I'm getting ready to go home. Listen. Find everything you can about a John Vanderhassen. He just died here at the hospital. Call the funeral homes. Find out if any service is scheduled. Get a home address. Have food catered to his widow, Emma. Get me the time of the service. And give the funeral home my credit card number. Tell them to charge all the expenses to me."

I want to use this new heart God has revived within me to comfort the broken heart of a new friend, Jack thought to himself as he hung up the phone. He couldn't remember feeling this good in a very long time.

Two days later, Jack went to John's funeral and sat alone at the back of the chapel. He had postponed his urgent business trip once again and scheduled a flight for the next day to visit his parents. An elderly cleric spoke a short, well-used eulogy over John Vanderhassen as his widow, Emma, sat weeping—alone—in the front pew.

After the benediction, Emma turned and saw Jack wiping away genuine tears. Surprised, she stood up and moved down the chapel's center aisle toward him. Their eyes met, and unspoken words passed between them. Jack stood and moved toward her.

An elderly widow and a reborn businessman, no longer strangers, their lives inextricably intertwined, met halfway down the aisle and embraced. Emma started to sob, burying her face in Jack's shoulder. He held her as though she were his mother, soothing her grief and praying silently.

Emma wept for a long time, tears of gratitude mingling with tears of sorrow. Time stood still, and Jack would have stayed there all day if that were what Emma required. Jack had all the time in the world for what was truly important, and this was. He would take her to the graveside and then out for dinner.

Emma didn't know it yet, but Jack had committed himself to check on her daily by phone. He would see that she was all right and visit her when she was lonely. Maybe someday he would keep a loving vigil by her bedside as her life slipped away. He would become like a real son to her—and to his own parents. His heart was so full and happy he wondered that his chest could contain it.

Heroes Go Beyond

Chapter 3

You are blessed when you persevere under trial. You're hard pressed on every side, but not crushed; perplexed, but not in despair; persecuted, but not abandoned; struck down, but not destroyed.

Your momentary trials are obtaining a glory that will definitely be worth all of your sacrifices. And remember...all things are possible with Me on your side.

LOVE,
YOUR GOD OF ALL COMFORT

—from James 1:12; 2 Corinthians 4:8–9, 17; Romans 8:18; Matthew 19:26

Most heroes, when applauded or commended for their heroism, simply exclaim, "I was only doing my job," or, "Anyone would have done what I did."

Perhaps that's true, but it still doesn't diminish the extraordinary effort and bravery demonstrated at a time of crisis or need. Heroes go beyond the ordinary and achieve the extraordinary. They grab hold of the impossible and do it. They go beyond what can be expected of them to sacrifice, invest, give, or do.

What empowers a hero to "go beyond"? An inner faith that sees the impossible as being possible. An inner love that puts others above self. An inner hope that believes that one person can make a difference in the world.

Heroes are simply ordinary people—like you—who do extraordinary things not because they have to but because God's power within lifts them beyond what's expected into the realm of the extraordinary and the miraculous!

Courage is not the absence of fear, but the capacity to move forward, confidently trusting the Maker of the heavens to cover us with the shadow of His mighty hand—even if the sky should fall.

—Susan Duke

When *Bill saw the flames leap out of Millie's window and engulf Jim, he raced up the ladder.*

Ladder Rescue

★ ★ ★ ★ ★ ★ ★ ★ ★ ★ ★ ★ ★ ★ ★

Millie woke up coughing. Her first thought was, *Not the flu again*. But then she smelled it. Smoke! She forced her eyes open. The deadly black intruder blanketed her room so thickly that she couldn't even see the door. She could feel the acrid smoke filling her lungs. Rising panic and smoke made breathing—difficult for Millie even on a good day—almost impossible. Ninety-one and confined to a wheelchair, Millie knew she didn't have the strength or mobility to outdistance the rapidly encroaching smoke and fire.

Would anyone come for her before it was too late? Millie was grateful she had fallen asleep watching television in her wheelchair and not in her bed. At least she was mobile should someone come to rescue her. But Millie had already come to the conclusion that no one could help her. She was all too aware that her rickety wooden home—even older than Millie herself—was a firetrap that should have been condemned years ago. It would have been, had there not been a shortage of retirement homes and nursing care centers in her small town of Smithton.

Smithton was a tiny dot on the map that had seen more prosperous days during the mining boom of the late 1800s. That was when the old five-story Smithton Hotel had been built from trees felled at the mine site. The old wooden structure had been updated a few times over the years with a new kitchen and an elevator that was less than reliable. But the building's quaint character and furnishings had gone largely unchanged since just after the Great Depression. That was perhaps the hotel's greatest appeal to its elderly residents—everything about the home reminded them of a time many years ago when they were young, hopeful, and just starting out. Now it was the Smithton Hotel's biggest danger.

These are my final moments, Millie thought with a strange combination of astonishment and acceptance. There was a tinge of sadness as she realized that no one was left to mourn her death. An only child who had never married, it had been years since Millie had been part of a family. *I've lived a long, good life, though,* Millie consoled herself with a touch of pride. She sank back into her wheelchair, squeezed her eyes tightly shut, then prayed. She was ready to die.

In the blackness that engulfed her consciousness, Millie was oblivious to the firehouse siren's blaring. But several streets away, two men Millie had never met heard it and swung instantly into action.

Bill and Jim had been volunteer firefighters in Smithton for more than ten years, but they'd been friends since their earliest school days. They had played ball together, double-dated, and they still attended the same Sunday school class. They worked together at the hardware store on Main Street: Bill owned the store, and Jim was his salesman and book-keeper.

When the siren rang, both ran out of the store and down to the end of the street. Small towns have some advantages, and the close proximity of Smithton's fire station to every building in town was one of them.

"I'll bet it's the old hotel," Bill shouted as they raced to meet the rest of the crew at the fire station.

"You're right," Jim pointed up to the part of the Smithton Hotel that could be seen beyond the single-story hardware store. "Look at the smoke pouring from those windows!"

The crew assembled in minutes, and the hook-and-ladder truck raced to the burning building. Handfuls of elderly residents and staff stood or sat in wheelchairs across the street. It was obvious that the entire building soon would be engulfed. Already the street-level entrances were blocked by blistering flames. Jim shuddered and hoped everyone had managed to escape.

But an agitated young woman dressed in white broke from the crowd and ran toward the firefighters. "Mildred Cox is still in there," she shouted to Jim. "She's on the fifth floor. We couldn't get to her room. The fire was too hot, and the stairway is filled with flames."

"I'm going up the ladder," Jim announced resolutely to Bill.

Bill positioned the ladder right below Millie's window, and Jim scurried up the rungs. At the top, he could only see black smoke filling the room. As soon as he broke the window with his axe, the outside air gave the internal blaze new life. Flames raced across the room, engulfing Jim in a roar of blistering heat.

Even with his mask, fire suit, and oxygen, Jim couldn't move forward. The fire blazed so fiercely that his only available path seemed to be back down the ladder. *No way I'm going back,* Jim thought. The fiery heat was now penetrating his suit, and smoke was beginning to seep through his mask. His eyes burning and swelling shut from smoke, his gloves burned through and his hands scorched, Jim lunged through the broken glass and onto the floor. It was ablaze like a charcoal grill.

The heat was so intense that Jim feared he'd never get out alive. He knew he only had seconds to locate the missing woman. Blinded by smoke, he could only feel his way through the room. Jim tripped. A bed. Feeling his way around the burning bed, he bumped into Millie's wheelchair. He reached for her. She wasn't in it!

Dropping to his hands and knees, Jim groped along the floor until he finally bumped into a human form. It was

Millie. She felt lifeless, but he couldn't stop to find out for sure. Lifting Millie over his shoulder, Jim crawled back toward the window. He couldn't stand up because flames from the ceiling made survival only possible a few inches off the floor—which itself was burning all around him.

By the time he neared the outside wall, Jim's mask was filled with smoke. His burned hands and knees made every movement torture. Millie's dead weight on his shoulder and back felt like a ton. Only grim determination drove him forward. Then the room swirled around him, and Jim collapsed…just inches from the window.

When Bill saw the flames leap out of Millie's window and engulf Jim, he raced up the ladder. At the top, the heat and smoke were so intense that he couldn't enter the room. "Jim!" he shouted at the top of his lungs. But there was no answer. No one could have been heard above the thunderous roar of the fire.

He couldn't go forward, but he wouldn't retreat. Bill felt helpless. He could think of nothing rational to do to save them. So he did something irrational. With all his strength, he threw himself into the flames and landed at the foot of the window. By sheer luck or God's grace, he landed right on top of Millie and Jim. Both were unconscious. Somehow, Bill managed to cradle Millie in his right arm while dragging Jim with his left. Draping Jim over the window sill, Bill carried Millie down the ladder to the waiting arms of the sheriff.

Looking back up, Bill saw something that sent a chill up his spine in spite of the overwhelming heat. The window frame over which Bill had draped Jim's limp body was now on fire around him. Bill ran back up the ladder and pulled Jim onto his shoulders. Immediately the whole window casing collapsed, leaving the ladder with the truck as its sole support as it swung free of the building. Carefully balancing himself and his precious cargo, Bill inched his way down the ladder, falling exhausted into the arms of waiting paramedics. Minutes later, from a safe distance across the street, Bill watched the entire building collapse.

Bill and Jim had gone above and beyond the call of duty on the day of the fire and definitely qualified as heroes. But their heroics didn't stop there. Millie was in the hospital for two weeks after the fire. Bill and Jim paid for all of her medical expenses. And every day, they stopped by to visit and check on her progress.

They discovered Millie had yet another problem. When she was ready to leave the hospital, she would have no place to go. With their home gone, the Smithton Hotel's other residents were staying with family or friends until a new retirement home could be built. But Millie had no family or friends.

The two men wanted to be Millie's heroes again. Jim had an extra bedroom at his house. Bill's and Jim's wives agreed to help the guys cook, clean, do laundry, and sit with Millie. Just a month after the fire, Millie moved in at Jim's and was adopted into a new, loving family.

Millie couldn't believe that anyone would do for her what Jim and Bill had done and continue to do. "I thought I was a goner," she tells everyone who will listen to her amazing story. "It looked like I had lost everything, but I gained something I never expected. Those boys are more than heroes to me...they're family!"

Heroes
Listen

Chapter

4

I've chosen you, giving you a new life! You are holy and dearly loved by Me. May compassion, kindness, humility, gentleness, and patience continue to be trademarks of your life.

I'm near anyone who calls on Me in truth. I hear your silent cries and rescue you. My law is perfect, reviving your soul. My statutes are trustworthy, making wisdom simple. My precepts are right, bringing joy to your heart. When you pursue righteousness and love, you'll find life, prosperity, and honor.

WITH ETERNAL LOVE,
YOUR GOD OF HOPE

—from Colossians 3:12; Psalms 145:18–19, 19:7–8;
Proverbs 21:21

Heroes have the uncanny ability to listen to the heart, not just to the spoken word. Anyone can refuse to listen, no matter how urgent the cry from someone's soul. But taking time to listen requires heroic effort.

How so? Listening means not interrupting another person's sharing. Listening means trying to understand. Listening conveys worth and importance to the speaker. Listening means taking time to really hear before leaping into a barrage of words that analyze or criticize.

This skill is a part of every hero's arsenal of weapons against apathy, ignorance, bigotry, and prejudice. Listening requires patient attentiveness.

Heroes have a unique ability to be quick to listen, slow to speak, and slow to anger. Heroes build bridges across the silent chasms that have kept others lonely and imprisoned in their private pain. By simply listening, heroes invite others to share without fear of rejection.

Wouldn't you like to encounter such a hero the next time you have something important or personal to share? Won't you aspire to be such a hero yourself?

To listen to someone
who has no one to
listen to him is a very
beautiful thing.

—Mother Teresa

Attentive *listening could build a bridge of understanding and acceptance that words never could.*

The Hero in 47B

★ ★ ★ ★ ★ ★ ★ ★ ★ ★ ★ ★ ★ ★ ★ ★

Valerie was looking forward to a quiet flight. Her plan for the cross-country trip was simple—sleep. Having worked late the night before, Valerie relished the thought of relaxing in seat 47B and sleeping until her plane started its descent into the Los Angeles airport.

Valerie's professional training had been in the field of family counseling. But after a few years of practice, she had decided that the stress of daily hearing other people's problems was too emotionally draining.

So Valerie had changed careers. Her training in personnel assessment and human resources had given her the skills to land a great-paying job as head of personnel in a prestigious firm. She enjoyed her nine-to-five job and the routine of administering tests she had developed and interviewing job candidates. Placing the right people in the right jobs gave Valerie great satisfaction.

A day rarely passed when she didn't feel grateful for her escape from her previous job and the world of other people's problems. She had counseled people with marital problems, rebellious teenagers, depressed and suicidal clients, and neurotics too paralyzed to make the simplest decisions.

She didn't miss it. The frantic, desperate, late-night phone calls had stopped. People expecting instant solutions to lifelong problems no longer sat in her office. No longer was it her responsibility to fix broken people. Her duty was to her company—to find healthy, capable, qualified workers.

Now it was time for a vacation. Valerie's family had flown to the West Coast a few days earlier. After a restful flight in solitude, Valerie planned to join them at Disneyland.

Much to her consternation, the flight was jammed full. Every seat was occupied, and Valerie found herself in an aisle seat, unable to stretch out beside a vacant spot as she had hoped.

At least I can nap, Valerie thought. She settled in and prepared to slip into pleasant dreams. Then she heard a quiet but distinct sniffle. Out of the corner of her eye, she noticed tears streaming down the face of the woman next to her. The woman was staring absently out the window, dabbing her eyes with a soggy tissue.

Sad about leaving her friend or husband, Valerie guessed, pushing down any inclination to speak to her. *She'll be over it in a few minutes,* she thought as she consciously willed herself to sleep.

But the sobbing didn't subside. In fact, what had started as a slow trickle of tears slowly intensified until she could feel the woman's sobbing shaking their seats.

I guess I should say something to comfort her, she thought. Bridging that initial gap with a stranger is never easy, but it's particularly hard when polite pleasantries simply don't fit. Her mind played over some of traditional opening lines for speaking to a stranger:

"How are you?"

"Nice day."

"What about this weather?"

"Are you going home?"

"Don't you just hate coach?"

But nothing easy was appropriate in this situation. Such platitudes simply don't work when the stranger you're about to address is sobbing uncontrollably.

Saying nothing would require callousness far beyond Valerie's weary reluctance. But saying the wrong thing could make things worse. She would have to be careful and play this by ear.

Valerie decided the best approach might simply be a statement that reflected the woman's own feelings without commentary or judgment. "I see you're crying," Valerie acknowledged quietly. "You seem very sad." Describing behavior and reflecting feelings was all Valerie wanted to do. She didn't really want to get involved. Part of her still hoped the woman would not want to talk and thus relieve her of her responsibility.

At first the woman said nothing, but her sobbing did begin to lessen. Valerie waited patiently. She didn't want to intrude, but she also wanted to convey understanding and empathy. Perhaps her presence, her tone, and her concern had soothed the woman enough to stop her tears and give Valerie what she wanted most—peace and quiet.

When the woman first spoke, it was so soft that Valerie almost missed it. She strained to catch the words. "My husband and I just filed for bankruptcy," the woman said, twisting several tissues tightly in her fingers as she spoke. "Our business, our beautiful home—everything's gone. He's driving a moving truck to my parents' home. We have to live with them now." Her face reflected her anguish, and her words started spilling out faster as she continued. "We've been married thirty years, raised two kids, and now we've lost everything. We have to start over again and move back in with my parents. I feel so humiliated."

She buried her head in her hands as if to hide her shame. "And we can't even be together. I wanted to drive with my husband, but I can't. I have to get back immediately to start a new job." She paused, then let out her last embarrassing secret. "It's in a fast-food restaurant. I've never worked outside the home. I have no job skills. I'm a mom, not a short-order cook."

61

Valerie said nothing. She just let her talk. She couldn't really change anything or help her, and any advice she could give would be meaningless. Cheerful hopefulness would seem shallow to a woman in such a dark place. But attentive listening could build a bridge of understanding and acceptance that words never could.

"I'm June," she said. She seemed suddenly embarrassed at what she had just told to a stranger, yet unquestionably relieved to have done so. "I don't know why I'm telling you all this," she told Valerie apologetically. "I guess it's easier to talk to a stranger than a friend—if I had one. It seems our friends have all deserted us. The only calls we've gotten in the last few months are from creditors and attorneys—all wanting something from us."

For the first time she really looked at Valerie and considered her as an individual, not merely a kind, listening ear. "I'm sorry," she said, realization dawning as she saw the pillow. "You must want to sleep."

"Don't worry about me," Valerie reassured her. "What's next for you?"

For more than two hours she listened to June's story. Occasionally, June would take a deep breath and sigh. Valerie would nod, murmur a quiet "Yes," and then listen as June continued her saga with new courage.

Valerie didn't sleep a wink on that late-night, cross-country flight. Her plans had changed. Her own needs had gone unmet, but she felt strangely refreshed and gratified that she had helped meet someone else's. She knew that listening to June was the most important thing she could have done. She was the right person at the right time and in the right seat—47B.

As the plane landed safely on the runway and taxied to the gate, June seemed relieved and even upbeat. "Your listening has meant so much to me," June sounded truly grateful. "I've had no one to talk to about anything important for such a long time. My husband and I are so weary of talking about what has happened and feel so powerless to change it that we often just sit for hours, staring at each other, feeling numb." She looked hopefully into Valerie's eyes. "So, what do you think?"

"I think you and your husband will make it," Valerie announced, suddenly quite confident of that. "It's a new beginning," she encouraged June. "Your past doesn't determine your future. Starting over can be a great thing."

With wide-eyed surprise, June looked at her traveling companion turned confidante. "I feel so much better," she said with a deep sigh of relief. "Thank you for listening. You'll never now how much this has meant to me. Without your intervention this would have been my last flight," she said solemnly, her eyes intense.

For the first time, Valerie's face registered that she didn't have a clue what June was talking about. So discreetly—ceremoniously—June reached into her purse and placed something into Valerie's hands. June closed her hand over Valerie's and gave it a brief but meaningful squeeze that wordlessly communicated her thanks and farewell. Valerie watched June sling her carry-on over her shoulder and walk down the aisle to the exit. She couldn't help but notice the change in June. She walked like a new woman with a new-found strength and courage.

Valerie watched her until she was gone, then opened her hand to examine what June had left with her. It was a small bottle of pills. She studied it curiously. The bottle contained sedatives—more than enough for a fatal overdose.

Sometimes a hero doesn't have to do much or risk a lot. Listening. Encouraging. Being there. Being willing. Such basic kindnesses don't seem like the daring acts of a hero. But at the right time, those qualities can change a stranger into a friend and enable an everyday hero to save a life.

Heroes
Carry
the Burden

Chapter

5

I've given you every grace and blessing you need for doing My will. Don't forget that your all-surpassing power is from Me and not from you.

I've saved you through My gift of grace. And My grace is all that you need. My power is perfected in your weakness. I'll make all grace abound to you so that you'll always overflow in every good work.

TESTIFY TO MY AMAZING GRACE,
JESUS

—from 1 Corinthians 1:7–9; 2 Corinthians 4:7;
Ephesians 2:8; 2 Corinthians 12:9, 9:8;
Acts 20:24

In life's endless struggles, victims complain and resent the burdens they must carry. Heroes, on the other hand, find the strength not only to carry their own burdens but also to pick up the load that is crushing someone else and carry it cheerfully.

What enables a hero to carry another's burden even when that load may seem impossibly overwhelming? Heroes discover that when they give of themselves to lift someone's burden, their own weariness melts away and their strength is multiplied to accomplish the extraordinary.

Burden-bearing is more than a rational, planned response to an obvious need. It's a miraculous equation God has established by which someone else's burden, no matter how heavy, is made light for another who will come alongside and lift it from his or her bowed-down shoulders.

Be a hero today. Help to carry a burden that is weighing someone down. You'll find it's not too heavy—and that your own burdens will feel lighter as well.

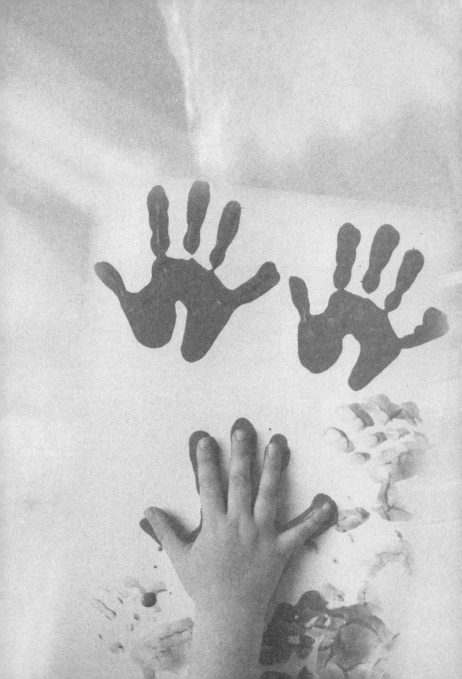

Manage them and our hands
become instruments of
grace—not just tools
in the hands of God, but
God's very hands.

—Max Lucado

Lee's surgeon addressed Chris after the successful surgery. "I don't know how you did it, but you saved your brother's life."

Strength of a Brother's Love

★ ★

The long, sultry, holiday weekend in July was marked by warm afternoon showers. But nothing seemed to dampen the spirits of the large crowd of music lovers at the festival on the Illinois State Fairgrounds. Country, bluegrass, southern gospel, and contemporary Christian music had delighted the enthusiastic crowd. Lee and his fellow band members had thoroughly enjoyed their gig. The added bonus was renewing old friendships with other bands, many of whom they only saw once a year at this festival.

Music was Lee's hobby. Now Sunday was fast disappearing, and Monday's approach brought thoughts of real-world responsibilities. Like every band member, Lee had a family and a job waiting back home in Georgia. He was due at work early Monday morning. His younger brother, Chris, had an early morning class. Visiting, eating, swapping stories, and playing music late into the previous two nights had been fun, but now everyone was tired and eager to get home. Happy but exhausted, the band loaded their trailer and prepared the fifteen-passenger rental van for the long drive home.

John, the group's manager, drew the first shift behind the wheel. He had gotten the most sleep the night before—four hours. Phil, the band's sound technician, rode shotgun. He would drive the second shift when John got tired. Five band members competed to be able to "stretch out" and sleep on one of the four bench seats on the eleven-hour ride home. The flip of a penny determined which unlucky musician would have to settle for a twin-sized foam mattress pad laid on the floor between two of the seats. After one last big dinner of fried chicken, they left the fairgrounds, settled into their assigned places, and headed toward home.

At first, the emotional euphoria of their exciting weekend

kept everyone awake, pumped up, and reliving memories. Even so, John decided it wouldn't hurt to pull through a nearby restaurant's drive-through for a large cup of coffee. As they waited in line to pick up the drink, the lack of sleep caught up with them. A profound but pleasant weariness settled on the passengers. By the time John pulled away from the drive-in window, everyone else was fast asleep.

John sipped his coffee, put on a favorite CD, and cranked up the sound and the air conditioning, hoping the combination of caffeine, noise, and cool air would make it easier to stay alert. He drove south on the interstate, determined to enjoy the drive as he sang along with familiar songs.

The first hour was uneventful. Traffic was unexpectedly light for a holiday weekend, and the scenery was pleasant but somewhat monotonous and mesmerizing. Tired of the CD, John searched the radio for some decent music or a controversial talk show. Finding neither, he turned off the radio and settled back into his own private musings.

Lost in thought, John tuned out the boredom of driving. He found himself on autopilot driving through some road construction. His alertness waned, and his drowsiness grew. *I need to pull over and let Phil drive for a while*, he thought.

He turned to ask Phil to relieve him, but his co-pilot was sleeping soundly, head buried in a pillow pressed against the window. When John looked back at the road, he realized the van had drifted toward the right edge. He quickly pulled the steering wheel to the left to correct his course.

But the construction had left the road's shoulder significantly lower than the driving lanes. The van's right front tire caught the edge of the pavement and, after a brief moment of resistance, overshot the road to the left shoulder. The van skidded left through the loose gravel strewn on the shoulder. John's adrenaline kicked in, and he jerked the van's steering wheel sharply to the right in a desperate and instinctive attempt to keep the unwieldy vehicle on the road. But the tire abruptly caught the pavement's edge at a speed of more than sixty miles per hour. By now the back trailer had begun to jackknife, making it impossible to control the van or even predict its movement.

Horrified, John was the only one awake to recognize their impending danger before the van and trailer rolled over in the wide, grassy median. The sleepers were jolted awake. Their unrestrained bodies flew through the air, impacting first one surface, then another. The grinding of metal and shattering of glass were deafening. Friction caused the smell of hot metal, and the air was thick with pulverized particles as the rolling van skidded upside down, windows popping out along the way.

And then it was over. The van teetered, then was motionless. For a moment the air was eerily silent, then there were moans of pain. Chris quickly evaluated his own condition, already aware of a multitude of bumps, bruises, and cuts. His right arm ached when he tried to move it, but he didn't appear to be seriously hurt. Immediately he thought of the others.

"Is everybody OK?" Chris shouted. Quickly he called out each band member's name. Three of the guys had neck injuries and hurt too much to move.

"I'm stuck here," Phil moaned. The van had come to rest on its passenger side. Phil's door was pinned shut by the ground, and his seat belt and the awkward position of his seat trapped him. John had been knocked unconscious and had a deep, bleeding gash on his forehead.

Everyone was accounted for except Chris's brother Lee. Chris shoved aside his own pain and rising panic. He knew he must find Lee and help him. With great effort, Chris pulled himself out of a bent and glassless window directly above his head on the driver's side. Sitting atop the overturned van, he felt a sharp pain in his right ankle. *I must have been slammed against the seat in front of me and really hurt my right arm and ankle,* Chris thought as he tried to clear the shock from his brain and focus on what he had to do.

"Lee! Lee, are you all right?" Chris shouted. No one answered. Ignoring the pain in his arm and ankle, Chris lowered himself to the grass. Dragging himself around the van, he searched for Lee.

Then he heard a weak moan from the ground near the back of the van. Chris moved toward the sound with both hope and dread. Hope was replaced by horror when he spotted his brother's arm under the van's right rear wheel. Lee had been thrown from the van and pinned beneath it.

Forgetting his own condition and the laws of physics, Chris stood and pushed against the massive van. It didn't budge.

"I can hardly breathe," Lee whispered with labored difficulty.

"Hold on," Chris pleaded.

Lee was a slender, six-foot, 160-pound rail of a guy who didn't have any fat to cushion him from the crushing weight of the van. Desperate, and with a strength far beyond himself, Chris used his good left arm to lift the wheel. In an instant, he grabbed Lee's extended arm with his own injured right arm. Screaming in pain, Chris lifted and pulled with more than everything in him. He felt consciousness slip away as he descended into total blackness.

The first rescue worker on the scene was a county sheriff. What he saw sickened him. He found five young men in the van and two lying on the grass about a yard away. All appeared seriously injured and by that time were unconscious.

When paramedics arrived, they rushed first to the broken and fragile-looking man lying near the van's rear tire. They revived Lee. "I...can't...breathe," Lee gasped, barely conscious. Recognizing the seriousness of Lee's condition, paramedics evacuated him and Chris by helicopter to the nearest major hospital.

During the fifteen-minute ride, Lee clung to life, barely breathing. Chris had come to and now directed his remaining strength toward encouraging his brother: "Lee, hang in there. I'm praying, bro. Don't give up."

At the hospital, Chris refused medical treatment for himself until he was sure he had done all he could for his brother. He learned that a broken rib had pierced Lee's left lung. The weight of the van had crushed his hip. He was bleeding internally. His spleen had ruptured. Lee was in serious condition, and Chris insisted on staying with him until doctors rushed his brother into surgery.

It was a miracle no one had been killed. The three men with injured necks would recover slowly over the next two months. John had a mild concussion and required stitches in his forehead. None had any serious or lasting injuries.

But when the details of what had happened were pieced together, there was little doubt there had been a second miracle. X-rays revealed that Chris had broken his ankle and right arm. Heroically, he had found the courage and strength to block out his pain, lift a fifteen-passenger van with one arm, and pull Lee out from under it with the other. Six paramedics, two police officers, and a sheriff had worked the accident scene. Trying to free Phil, who was trapped inside, these nine men had tried to accomplish what Chris had somehow managed by himself. But they couldn't. It took a tow truck to lift the van off its side and free Phil.

"Son," Lee's surgeon addressed Chris after the successful surgery. He shook his head in amazement at the young man on crutches with casts on his arm and leg. "I don't know how you did it, but you saved your brother's life. If he had been left under that van until the rescuers arrived, he surely would have suffocated to death."

That day, an ordinary man reached down inside and found something extraordinary to help his brother in need. More than his brother's keeper, Chris became his brother's hero!

Heroes
Are
Courageous

Chapter
6

Never fear people or circumstances, for I am with you! I'll strengthen you and help you.

I'll uphold you with My righteous right hand. Don't be overcome by evil. Instead, take a stand, overcoming evil with good. I'm your guide, even to the end.

FEAR ONLY ME,
YOUR ALMIGHTY GOD

—from Isaiah 41:10; Romans 12:21; Psalm 48:14

Life is filled with tests. Those tests are opportunities for powerful testimonies to God's faithfulness to grant us the strength and courage necessary to overcome every obstacle and to finish strong. A hero's courage is demonstrated in the midst of danger and crisis. Heroes refuse to avoid life's confrontations with evil. Rather, heroic courage faces the test, resolutely attacks every obstacle, and perseveres to the best of its ability.

Perhaps the greatest battle each hero must fight is against discouragement. An impending crisis or trial threatens defeat. Cowards cower before the enemy and retreat. The weak crumble under attack. Discouragement causes its victims to falter, believing all is lost.

But heroes know that with God, nothing is impossible. They believe they can overcome in spite of overwhelming odds. Armed with the indomitable weapon of courage, heroes march into battle convinced that the battle is worth any cost or sacrifice. Such men and women stand firm and serve as examples who inspire others to carry on with courage.

Courage is the strength to
face pain, act under pressure,
and maintain one's values in
the face of opposition.

—Eleanor Roosevelt

The *sergeant didn't seem to notice the danger of the spot, only the wounded man's great need.*

Courage under Fire

★ ★ ★ ★ ★ ★ ★ ★ ★ ★ ★ ★ ★ ★ ★ ★ ★ ★ ★ ★

Private First Class Keith Rodriguez gripped his M-16 rifle tighter. He heard nothing but the roar of the engine and chopping of the CH-53 "Super Jolly Green Giant's" whirring rotor blades. It was just like dozens of training exercises he had been on, yet it was nothing like those flights. This was no training exercise. This was a real mission.

Fresh out of boot camp, this would be twenty-year-old Rodriguez's first combat mission. A jumble of conflicting thoughts and emotions fought for his attention. Did he want to be here, or didn't he? This was the culmination of all he had trained for. When the United States had pulled out of Vietnam two weeks earlier and Saigon had fallen to the North Vietnamese, the war had been officially declared over. That meant PFC Rodriguez would never have to fight in the Vietnam conflict.

He remembered feeling an immediate sense of relief, but he had also felt oddly disappointed. After all the months of training, what sort of soldier would he have made? Would he have frozen in fear? Or would he have had the stuff of heroes—courage and grace under fire?

Now it looked as if Rodriguez would find out. The SS *Mayaguez*, a merchant vessel sailing under the American flag, had been boarded and captured by Cambodia's new Khmer Rouge regime. Its crew had been removed from the ship and whisked away to a secret location. Rodriguez and nineteen fellow marines, two navy medics, and the chopper's air force crew were on their way to that location—Koh Tang Island—to rescue the crew of the *Mayaguez* in a daring surprise raid.

Eight choppers loaded with men and weapons were to take part in the mission. Intelligence indicated that the island was not well fortified or defended—they expected to encounter no more than twenty to forty enemy soldiers. The marines would greatly outnumber the Cambodian fighters, and resistance was expected to be light. Still, Rodriguez had an uneasy feeling. His mouth was dry, his palms sweaty no matter how many times he wiped them on his standard-issue life jacket. *Just nerves,* he told himself. *It's completely normal. Nothing will go wrong. Please, God, help nothing to go wrong,* he prayed.

The trip lasted an eternity, and it was over all too soon. Rodriguez looked at his watch as they began their sunrise descent onto the east side of Koh Tang Island. It was just a few minutes after 0600. *Protect me, God,* Rodriguez prayed silently. *Give me courage.* He could feel his muscles grow taut in anticipation of disembarking from the safety of the chopper and heading up that exposed beach to the cover of the jungle.

Rodriguez never got that chance. Without warning, the mission spun out of control. A hail of antiaircraft mortar rounds pierced the belly of the chopper before it could land. The CH-53 pulled up and turned back sharply, its air force crew struggling valiantly to save the chopper and those it carried. Men and weapons tumbled helplessly inside the belly of the wounded giant. Stoic marines cried out in shock and pain. Blood exploded from a handful of bullet wounds from the initial volley. Other men were hurt when they were thrown against the side of the helicopter in its violent maneuverings. Some were injured when they were hit by flying bodies and weapons.

Then there was another massive shudder accompanied by the horrible sound of an explosion. Flames quickly engulfed the helicopter as it stalled and plunged downward in a crash landing. But this was not land. Stunned and terrified, Rodriguez was overcome suddenly by a rush of seawater. Instinctively he spat out the water, but he inhaled just enough to leave him choking and gasping for air. The air he drew into his irritated lungs was filled with smoke. It was dark inside, so dark. The bumping and roiling of the chopper had turned Rodriguez's sense of direction upside down. He had no idea which direction, if any, would lead to escape.

Utter confusion and terror reigned inside the chopper. The men could hear more machine-gun fire outside. The water was rising. The smoke was growing thicker. They could hear the flames raging ever closer and feel the approaching heat. Even the seawater was growing warmer. Rodriguez looked around. Surely one of them would know what to do. But no one stepped forward. Any action, any direction, seemed as deadly as any other.

Suddenly a lone figure broke through the flame and smoke into the belly of the chopper. It was an air force staff sergeant, one of the CH-53's crew. He held his arm across his face to shield it from the flames and smoke, but he dropped it long enough to shout to the men: "You've got to get out of here now! This way. Follow me."

A thrill of relief and gratitude overwhelmed Rodriguez. Finally a direction, instructions. A way out. Those who were not dead or mortally wounded were glad to follow this man who had risked flames and water for their sake. *What sort of man is this?* Rodriguez wondered as he noted that not even a bullet wound through the leg had stopped this man from coming to the aid of the privates and lance corporals in the back.

Rodriguez could feel his skin burning and his hair singeing as he broke through the wall of fire to the blown-open front of the chopper. As soon as he felt the heat diminish and sensed sunlight through his tightly closed eyelids, he gulped a huge breath of air. It was still smoky, but he could also smell and taste the sea and the island air. *Thank You, God!* Rodriguez prayed with great feeling.

Then reality struck him again. The staff sergeant pushed him off of the burning chopper into the water. "Stay down," he commanded. "We're under fire from the beach. Our only hope is to swim out to sea beyond range of their weapons. Swim, boys, swim for your lives. They'll come for us soon!"

His heart pounding, his lungs burning, his left arm aching from some undetermined injury, Rodriguez was happy to comply. Along with half a dozen other mobile marines, he swam with all his might. But he paused for a moment in the shadow of the dying helicopter, protected from bullets by its hulking, burning frame. His fear was momentarily superseded by admiration and awe for the courageous hero who had led the marines safely from the burning wreckage.

The man was air force. He had probably never even met any of the young marines or navy medics he had saved. Yet his heroism didn't end there. Rodriguez saw him disappear into the burning chopper one more time, emerge with more wounded marines and an M-16 rifle, then lay down covering fire to protect the retreat of the dazed and injured men. He stood his ground until he had exhausted all the ammunition, then plunged into the surf to head to sea.

Rodriguez knew he had to swim out to sea, but the water scared him almost as much as the attack from the beach. He imagined himself being pulled far out to sea, out of sight of the rescue choppers. There was a lot of blood in the water, and he knew there were sharks. He mused that being shot would be preferable to being torn and eaten.

As he clung to the chopper, working up his strength and courage for the swim, he noticed that the staff sergeant had picked up a wounded marine struggling to stay afloat and was swimming toward Rodriguez.

Suddenly Rodriguez heard a pained, fearful cry for help. It was coming from the other side of the chopper—the side dangerously exposed to sniper fire. The staff sergeant heard it too and resolutely altered his course toward it. The first wounded marine clung to his rescuer's webbing, slowing his progress.

Rodriguez shifted to where he could see the source of the cries for help. It was a badly wounded marine. He was burned and in great pain. But perhaps his greatest fear stemmed from the fact that he had been blinded. He couldn't see danger or the way to safety. The tumultuous world of blackness and sounds had rooted him in fear to his dangerous spot.

But the sergeant didn't seem to notice the danger of the spot, only the wounded man's great need. As he stood up to reach out to the man, he was hit hard by enemy fire. One round slammed into his helmet, knocking him momentarily senseless. Additional rounds ripped away most of his life jacket but amazingly missed his body. Shaking his head clear to recover, the man grabbed the blinded marine and launched himself toward deeper water. With almost no assistance from his life preserver or from either injured man, the sergeant steadfastly made his way out to sea.

The man's commitment never wavered, but his strength did. Suddenly the sergeant's heroism gripped Rodriguez's heart. Heedless of the personal danger, he swam alongside the struggling trio. His own life preserver was intact, and he selflessly offered it—along with his assistance—to the wounded hero and his charges.

Aching muscles and tortured lungs later, they were finally out of range of Khmer Rouge snipers. A ragged band of just thirteen men bobbed up and down on the waves; thirteen others had been lost.

The men were silent—numb—as they waited three hours for their rescuers, but Rodriguez saw many pain-filled eyes look with respect and gratitude toward the courageous staff sergeant who had saved their lives.

Rodriguez's mind was an overwhelming jumble of conflicting thoughts and feelings. But standing out among them was a sense of satisfaction and pride. He had been privileged to see true bravery and heroism. Even more important, this hero had inspired those actions in himself. Now he knew what he was made of. He would face whatever life would throw at him with grace and courage.

Heroes Take Notice

Chapter 7

Your lifestyle of selfless service to others is making you great in My eyes! A good life and deeds done in humility showcase your wisdom and understanding. As you humble yourself, I'm promoting you.

I'll reward your actions as you serve others as if you're serving Me. And as you continue to give, I'll generously bless you with much more than you invested.

CHEERING YOU ON TO LOVE AND GOOD DEEDS,
YOUR SERVANT JESUS

—from Mark 10:43–45; James 3:13, 4:10;
Ephesians 6:7–8; Luke 6:38

Some people can pass by others in need and never even see them. The masses rush past without pausing to notice or taking time to care. It's as though they don't exist.

But heroes stop and take notice. They see the unpopular, unappreciated, sometimes unlovely people around us. Heroes find needs and meet them, understand hurts and heal them.

Heroes aren't concerned with rewards or recognition. Instead of wanting to be seen, they see others through a singular scope of clarity. Heroes know that hurting people are not statistics but individuals who need love and care.

Are you a hero? Take notice today of the people you normally pass without a thought. How many of them are lonely or sad or in need? What can you do to help? You don't have to fix every problem. Heroes rarely help everyone. What distinguishes heroes from the crowd is the willingness to notice what others choose to ignore—individual souls, each created and loved by God, who are valuable and who just might need a hero today.

I am only one,
But still I am one.
I cannot do everything,
But I can still do something;
And because I
cannot do everything
I will not refuse to do the
something which I can do.

—Edward E. Hale

That *night Megan* snuggled up in her favorite blanket, wrapping it around her tightly. Suddenly she sat up. "That's it!"

A Blanket Statement

* *

Megan's excitement grew by the minute as she brushed her hair in preparation for her biggest date of the year. Two or three times a month, twelve-year-old Megan and her dad, Ted, would have a "date"—a special father-daughter outing. Sometimes they went to see a movie, other times to a favorite restaurant or ice cream parlor. But Megan's favorite kind of outing was shopping.

Shopping took half a day. Megan got to visit all her favorite stores in the mall, and her dad would let her try on outfit after outfit as he patiently waited for her ongoing fashion show. But today was special—her favorite shopping trip of the year. This was their Christmas shopping trip.

Instead of going to the nearby mall, Megan and her father would take the subway into the city. Megan loved the elaborate Christmas decorations and the huge department stores. She was mesmerized by one massive floor-to-ceiling tree loaded with twinkling lights and sparkling ornaments.

Megan had saved her baby-sitting money and allowance to buy gifts for her family. Then, after shopping all afternoon, she and her dad would eat at a classic downtown diner, go to an early Christmas movie, and ride the subway back home laden with gifts and priceless memories.

Everything was just as fun and festive as Megan had anticipated. But the stores were so crowded and the prices so high that she only found a few gifts that she both liked and could afford. *No matter,* she thought. *In a few days, I'll just go with Mom to some local stores for the rest of the gifts.* The experience of Christmastime downtown was worth the crowded bustle. She still had most of her money to find some really nice presents later. So Megan and her dad set off for their favorite diner and enthusiastically ate huge, juicy burgers while they deliberated over which Christmas movie to see.

Suddenly Megan glanced out the diner window and squealed. "Dad, look! This is just perfect. It's beginning to snow!" Light, powdery flakes drifted lazily and began coating the city in a magical white Christmas blanket. Megan was glad they had checked the weather forecast and dressed warmly, as the temperature had dropped swiftly into the low twenties.

As Megan hung on to her dad with one hand and carried two shopping bags in the other, the two raced out of the diner and down the four blocks toward the theater. Warm air from the subway below rose up through the grates in the sidewalks and formed clouds of steam as it hit the cold, wintry air. Megan was enjoying the city sights when she felt her right foot bump something and heard a moan escape from a formless heap.

Startled, Megan stopped and tugged her dad back to the creature she had kicked. Lying bundled in a tattered coat and covered with newspapers was one of the city's many homeless people who found some small warmth by sleeping on the subway grates when the nights grew cold.

"I'm sorry to have kicked you, sir," Megan apologized.

"Don't worry about him," her dad said as he nudged her

away. "Let's move on and not disturb him." The man simply moaned again and turned over, ignoring them.

Megan took her dad's hand, and they moved on toward the theater. But the show that night failed to capture Megan's attention. All she could think about was the shivering, homeless man with nothing to shelter him but a few newspapers.

"You're awfully quiet," Ted commented as they headed home on the subway. "Still thinking about that homeless man we stumbled onto?" he asked.

Tears welled up in Megan's eyes. "Dad, isn't there anything we can do to help? After all, it's Christmas, and it's really cold."

"What do you suggest?" Ted asked. Megan thought hard all the way home, but the situation seemed hopeless. What could a twelve-year-old do about the city's homeless population?

When Megan and her dad arrived home, her mom and brother greeted them cheerfully and asked about their excursion, but the father and daughter were subdued. They relayed what had happened, but no one seemed hopeful that anything could be done to help the situation.

That night Megan snuggled up in her favorite blanket, wrapping it around herself tightly. Suddenly she sat up. *"That's it!"* she thought. Jumping out of bed, she snatched the blanket and ran into the family room where her mom and dad were watching television.

"Dad! Mom! I know what we can do!" Megan exclaimed. "Let's get all of our blankets together and give them to those homeless people. At least they'll be warmer on the cold nights!"

Megan's parents gave several reasons why handing out a few blankets wouldn't do much good and explained that it could be dangerous. But Megan persisted. She collected the rest of her Christmas money and vowed to buy more blankets with it. As she argued her case, the late-night local news forecasted single-digit temperatures and at least twelve inches of snow by morning. "We've got to go back tonight," Megan pleaded. "Some of those people could freeze without our blankets."

Something about Megan's innocent yet convicting plea touched her parents' hearts. Though they knew it was impractical, they gave in and gathered all the blankets they

115

could find. Most stores were closed at that hour, but the family stopped at a local Wal-Mart so Megan could purchase a few more blankets.

The travelers were quite a sight—a middle-class, suburban family of four, carrying a dozen blankets on an hour-long, late-night subway trip to the inner city. When they finally arrived at the stop near the theater, Megan raced to the top of the stairs toward the grate. The man was still there, trying to sleep and huddling for warmth with another man who had crowded in on his grate. Megan's family caught up with her just as she covered the first man with her blanket and reached for another for the second man.

Two blankets distributed, ten to go. Megan saw two more men covered with cardboard boxes and sleeping against a building. As she approached, one of the men jumped up, cursed the family, and took off down the street with his box in hand. The other man didn't move, and Megan wasn't about to be deterred. She fearlessly covered the other sleeping transient with a blanket while her dad stood guard.

Nine more blankets left to give away. Turning back toward the street, they were surprised to come face to face with two police officers. "What are you doing?" one of them demanded to know. "You could get yourselves mugged out here like this!"

Ted patiently explained what they were doing while the second officer went to the patrol car to give a report. "I don't think this is such a safe idea," the first officer cautioned.

"But they could freeze without the blankets!" Megan pleaded tearfully. "I've spent all of my Christmas money on these new blankets. I have to give them away before it's too late for someone." Touched by the girl's compassion and determination, the officers decided to follow a few paces behind the family as an informal escort for their mission of mercy.

Unknown to any of them, a local television news team in a remote broadcast van had picked up the unusual police report on their scanner. Now they pulled alongside the curb just as the young hero found another homeless man sleeping on a subway grate and carefully covered him with a blanket.

The news team recorded the young girl's crusade to make a small but important difference for a few homeless people.

When interviewed, Megan told of the need for homeless people to have blankets on such a cold night.

Early the next morning, Megan's mission was broadcast on the local news. A network morning show also aired a brief segment on Megan's efforts, and her plea struck a nerve in the national audience. Calls flooded in, and overnight, TV stations became the depositories for people donating blankets for the homeless. Local street missions and homeless shelters also picked up the crusade.

Over the next week, Megan's plea was rebroadcast again and again. Her one-person crusade launched a movement throughout her city and in other urban areas to provide blankets and aid to the homeless. Thousands of them received blankets, food, and shelter during that icy Christmas season…all because one girl took notice and refused to ignore another person's need.

Journal

* * * * * * * * *

Write your own story of a hero who has "hugged" your life and deserves to be celebrated. Then share your story with your hero to express your heartfelt thanks.

_____

_____

_____

_____

_____

_____

_____

_____

_____

_____

_____

_____

_____

_____

_____

_____

_____

_____

_____

_____

_____

_____

_____

_____

_____

_____

_____

_____

_____